Stained Glass
Flower Garden

by

Brenda Henning

Bear Paw Productions

PO Box 230589 • Anchorage, AK 99523-0589
(907) 349-7873 • Phone   (907) 349-7875 • FAX
www.bearpawproductions.com

Dedication

To my children - there is never a dull moment, and the car engine is never cold.

Acknowledgments

Many thanks to Norma Kindred. She took time out of her busy life to quilt the Stained Glass Flower Garden. Her generosity allowed the book to be ready on schedule.

Credits

Written and illustrated by Brenda Henning.
Edited by Marcia Harmening.
Photography by Randy Brandon,
        Third Eye Photography.
Printed in the United States of America.

ISBN 0-9648878-3-5

Stained Glass Flower Garden©
©1998 by Brenda Henning
Bear Paw Productions
PO Box 230589
Anchorage, AK 99523-0589
Phone (907) 349-7873
FAX   (907) 349-7875
www.bearpawproductions.com

Introduction

We surround ourselves with beautiful things in an effort to soothe our souls, tattered by busy, eventful lives. Flowers have the power to touch us deep within. Just the scent of a flower will bring us back to a moment long forgotten.

Table of Contents

General Directions

I hope that you will take the time to read through this first chapter before cutting fabrics. I realize that many of you are experienced in the ways of quilting and do not have any need to be told how to cut your fabric. You will find that many of the questions you might have about my approach to piecing will be answered in the following pages.

The yardage listed has been rounded up slightly to allow for the fact that the scrap approach used to make this quilt tends to use more fabric than one would normally use.

Yardage has been based upon 42" wide fabric. If your fabric is substantially wider or narrower after prewashing, your yardage requirement may also need adjustment.

1/4" seams are used throughout the piecing. The cutting instructions given for each piece refer to the actual cut size. The 1/4" seam allowance has been added to all dimensions. Check the accuracy of your seams before you begin. You will find a simple "1/4" seam test" in the following pages. Accuracy is important to the success of your quilt. This quilt includes a pieced border. The piecing of the body of the quilt will determine if the border fits properly! The measurements given are all mathematically correct, it is assumed that your piecing will also be correct.

Cutting instructions assume that all strips are cut the width of the fabric, measured selvage to selvage. This strip should measure 42" or longer. Do not cut the strip to this length.

Half square and quarter square triangle units are made from layered fabric squares using **triangle foundation papers**. The triangle foundation paper method allows for accurate results. Master foundation papers have been provided on page 30. You may trace or photocopy the number of foundations that you need. Triangle foundation papers are also available preprinted. Check with your local quilt shop for availability. Standard cutting instructions have been included for those who choose to use traditional methods.

Fabric Preparation

Fabric preparation should be handled in the same manner that the quilt will be cared for when completed. I recommend prewashing all fabrics. As each piece enters my house, the first stop is the laundry room. All fabric in my personal stash has been washed using Orvus paste (a horse shampoo) or Dreft. Do not use detergent to wash your cotton fabrics because detergents act to strip color from cotton fabrics.

To replace the firmness of the sizing that has been washed out of the fabric, press all fabrics using a heavy spray starch or spray sizing. The fabric that is prepared in this way will behave much better when pressing seams. Bias edges will be more stable and less likely to stretch. You will find that piecing is much easier with fabric that doesn't stretch out of shape so quickly.

Rotary Cutting Tools

The rotary cutter is a razor knife that resembles a pizza cutter. The blade is very sharp and deserves to be treated with utmost respect. This amazing tool has revolutionized quilt making, nearly replacing scissors. I recommend a rotary cutter that has a manual safety guard. Some rotary cutters available on the market have a spring-loaded guard that can accidentally retract when dropped, exposing the razor sharp blade and cutting your hand or foot. The spring-loaded guards protect you from only the most minor of blade "bumps." The rotary cutters that have a manually closing safety guard, such as Olfa® and Fiskar®, require that you consciously close the guard after every cut. Learn to make a habit of closing the guard every time!! An exposed blade on the work surface can lead to tragic results, accidentally cut fabric or worse — cut fingers and bloodstained fabric. Do not leave a rotary cutter unattended around a curious toddler or young child.

I prefer to use the Olfa® rotary cutter. This particular rotary cutter can be used both right and left-handed without repositioning the blade.

To ensure the life of the blade, the rotary cutter must be used only on a compatible cutting surface. The self-healing cutting mats are a necessary tool. While the mats come in many sizes, purchase the largest cutting mat that you can afford. The 24" x 36" cutting mat is worth every dime.

Omnigrid® is my ruler of choice. The Omnigrid® brand is the most accurate of all rulers that I have worked with. It is very important that all of your rulers are accurate and agree with each other. Compare the markings of all rulers in your collection. If any ruler does not measure up, discard it!! The markings on your rotary mat must also agree with the rulers you have chosen to use.

Squaring Up Yardage

•Fold your fabric in half lengthwise, wrong sides together, selvage edges even. You may need to shift one selvage to the right or left to eliminate wrinkles along the folded edge. Once this has been accomplished, fold the fabric again, lengthwise, bringing the folded edge even with the selvage edges. The fabric will now be folded into four thicknesses, and measure about 10 1/2" wide. Fabric folded to this width can be cut into strips without repositioning your ruler hand.

•Lay the folded fabric horizontally on your gridded cutting mat. The folded edge should be nearest you. Place the fold along a horizontal line of the mat. This will allow you to place your ruler along a vertical mat marking, guaranteeing a straight cut. If you are right-handed, the bulk of your fabric should

be on the right, and you will start cutting from the left side. This will be reversed for a left-handed person.

•The rotary cutter is held with the blade perpendicular to the mat and against the edge of the ruler. If the blade is held at any other angle, the cutting will not be as effective and effortless. The rotary cutter is held in the palm of your hand with the index finger on the ridged surface of the handle. This placement helps you to better control the rotary cutter. You are in effect pointing it in the proper direction.

•Cut away from yourself using one smooth even stroke. Do not make short choppy cuts which will create a ragged edge. The first cut will trim off the raw edge and square up the fabric. The clean edge will be perpendicular to the selvage. Trim sparingly to give the fabric a clean edge while wasting as little fabric as possible.

Cutting Strips

After the original cut has been made to square up the end of the yardage, you are ready to cut your first strip.

•Move the ruler to the right (left for a left-handed person) and align the newly cut edge with the ruler marking for the strip width desired. Make sure that the correct marking lines up all along the cut edge, not just at one point!! Measure twice and cut once!!

•Cut along the right (left) side of the ruler. Be sure to keep your blade flush against the ruler, do not allow the ruler to shift. It may be helpful to hold the ruler with a finger or two off the left (right edge for a left-handed person) edge. This will stabilize the ruler a help to prevent ruler slips. Lift the ruler and remove the strip without disturbing the yardage.

•Open the strip and look at it closely. The strip should be straight and of a consistent width. If your strip is not straight, refold your fabric and make certain that the edges are even. Also, make sure the original cut was made correctly, perpendicular to the folded edge.

•If it is necessary to cut a strip wider than your ruler, use the rulings of the cutting mat to measure the strip or square. Double check the mat measurements against those of your ruler to determine if the mat measurements are accurate.

Subcutting Strips

•Squares and rectangles needed for piecing will be cut from strips. Cut the strip to the required width and open the double fold. You will be working with two layers of fabric and a single fold. If you are right handed, the selvages should be placed at the left. Trim off the first 1/2" to remove the selvages (more if needed) and square up the end of the strip. Use the mat markings to establish a perpendicular cut.

•Align the bottom edge of the fabric with a horizontal ruler marking. Cut the squares or rectangles to the required dimension. Continue cutting from the strip to satisfy the number needed.

Cut Once Diagonally

Fabric pieces that will be used as individual half square triangles will be cut as squares with the instructions to cut each square once diagonally as diagramed below. Cutting a square once diagonally places the stretchy bias edge along the long side of the triangle.

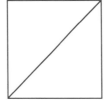 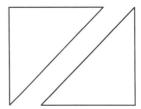

Cut Twice Diagonally

Fabric pieces that will be used as individual quarter square triangles will be cut as squares with the instructions to cut each square twice diagonally as diagramed below. Cutting a square twice diagonally places the stretchy bias edge along the two short sides of the triangle.

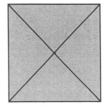 

Machine Piecing

1/4" Seam Allowance

All of our seams will be sewn with a 1/4" seam allowance. It is of utmost importance to establish and maintain an accurate 1/4" seam allowance. Some of you will already have quilting experience and feel confident that you know where your 1/4" seam is. I would encourage you to do the following exercise anyway. I find that many of my students have misjudged their seam allowance and have been able to correct it with this exercise.

You will actually be sewing with a **scant** 1/4" seam allowance. The difference will be taken up in the slight fold or "ridge" at the seam.

•To find your 1/4" seam allowance place a small ruler underneath your presser foot. When the needle is gently lowered, it should rest just to the right of the 1/4" mark on the right side of your ruler. If the needle were to pierce the ruler, the hole left by the needle would just graze the 1/4" marking on your ruler.

•With the presser foot holding the ruler in this position, carefully adjust the ruler so the markings on the left side of the ruler run parallel with the markings on the throat plate of your sewing machine.

•Once you are satisfied the ruler is positioned correctly, place a 1/2" x 3" strip of moleskin along the right edge of the ruler on the throat plate. Moleskin is a Dr. Scholl's® product, available at most groceries and pharmacies. The adhesive back of the moleskin will stick to the throat plate and give an edge to hold your seam allowance against. Moleskin gives more of an edge to follow than masking tape. It is not high enough that it will impede or pull out your pins.

1/4" Seam Test

•Cut 3 pieces of fabric 1 1/2" x 6". Sew these strips together along the lengthwise edge. Press the seams in one direction. After pressing, check that there are no "accordion" pleats at the seams. Press again if necessary.

•Measure your sewn unit, it should measure exactly 3 1/2" from raw edge to raw edge. The strips on either side should measure 1 1/4", and the center strip should measure 1" wide.

•If your sewn unit doesn't measure exactly 3 1/2", you will need to adjust your moleskin. If the sewn unit is **wider** than 3 1/2", your seam allowance is too narrow and the moleskin should be moved to the right. If the sewn strip is **narrower** than 3 1/2", your seam allowance is too wide and the moleskin should be moved to the left.

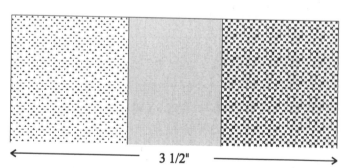

The amount that you need to move the moleskin is only one fourth of the amount that your strip differs from 3 1/2". Two seams are involved in the sewn strip, each seam involves two pieces of fabric - move the moleskin 1/4 of the difference.

It is a commonly held thought that the 1/4" seam allowance should be measured to check the accuracy of the stitching. Unfortunately, this does not work. The seam allowance is a scant 1/4". Measure the finished dimension of the fabric from the right side of the unit or quilt block.

I do not trust the 1/4" marking on my sewing machines. Usually the factory markings are accurate enough for clothing construction, but not for the precision demanded by quilting. I also do not recommend using the edge of your presser foot as a guide. Very few actually measure 1/4" from the needle.

If you have placed the moleskin exactly as described, and are still having problems stitching a 1/4" seam allowance, it may be your sewing machine that is being naughty. The feed dogs of some machines pull to the right, some to the left. Sewing machines are an eccentric lot! Adjust the moleskin to where the sewing machine demands that the edge of the fabric be held. This may not be at the mark 1/4" from the needle. Get to know your machine and work with its character flaws.

Chain Piecing

Chain piecing refers to the practice of stitching units one right after another without clipping the threads between the units. The first unit is stitched and left attached to the threads after passing under the presser foot. The second and following units are inserted under the presser foot one or two stitches after the previous unit has passed. No threads are cut.

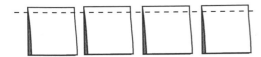

This method saves thread and the time required to start each unit as an individual. It also allows you to repetitively piece the same unit and create a rhythm, thereby reducing mistakes. Once the required number are stitched, remove the strip from the sewing machine and separate the units.

Triangle Foundation Paper

Half Square Triangles

Half square triangles are one of the most basic shapes used in quiltmaking. Unfortunately, they are also one of the most often distorted shapes. Gridded

triangles have long been present in quilting instructions. The use of ridded paper foundations greatly increases accuracy. Master triangle foundations may be found on pages 30-31. If you would prefer to use commercially prepared papers, refer to the sources listed on page 32, or check with your local quilt shop for availability.

• Photocopy or trace the number of triangle papers necessary.

• Cut the fabrics as indicated in the individual pattern. The square cut will be slightly larger than the paper foundation.

• Place two fabric pieces right sides together. Position a triangle paper on the **wrong side of the background fabric** and pin the paper to the fabric pair.

• Starting at the dot, stitch on all dotted lines. Follow the numbered arrows for a continuous seam. Use a small stitch (15 - 20 stitches per inch), and a size 14 sewing machine needle, to better perforate the paper foundation.

• Cut on all solid lines using a rotary cutter and ruler. Each 6 1/4" pair will yield 8 2" (finished size) half square triangle units.

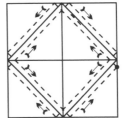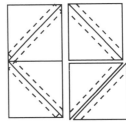

• With the paper still attached, press the seam toward the dark fabric.

• Remove the paper foundation. Place your thumb nail on the stitched seam at the center of the block. Pull the paper foundation from the square corner against your thumb nail. This will help to reduce the number of stitches lost at the seam ends.

• Trim all dog ears.

Quarter Square Triangles

Quarter square triangles are also often maligned. Gridded quarter square triangle paper is also available commercially. Master foundation papers can be found on page 30 if you would rather trace or copy an original. Quarter square triangle papers are used in the same way you would use half square triangle papers.

• Place two fabric pieces right sides together. Position a triangle paper on the **wrong side of the background fabric** and pin the paper to the fabric pair.

• Stitch on all dotted lines. Cut on all solid lines using a rotary cutter and ruler.

• With the paper still attached, press the seam toward the dark fabric.

• Remove the paper and trim all dog ears.

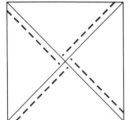 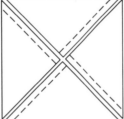

Foundation Paper Piecing

Points To Remember

• Each master foundation is meant to be used as a pattern to create the foundation papers that you will stitch through. A photocopied foundation may be distorted. Always compare the copy to the master, and make all copies needed from the same machine. If the copy varies significantly from the original, discard the copy and try a different copying machine.

• It is helpful to use a larger sewing machine needle, such as a size 14 needle.

• Stitch with a shorter stitch length, 15 - 20 stitches per inch, to better perforate the paper.

• The lines on the pattern are the actual sewing lines. Sew directly on these lines.

• The fabric pieces will be placed on the **unmarked** side of the foundation paper, and the seam will be sewn from the marked side.

• The fabric pieces do not need to be cut precisely. After stitching, the excess will be trimmed to a 1/4" seam allowance. Take care to allow sufficient fabric to cover the area.

• Each block is diagramed with the numerical sequence of fabric application.

• The foundation pattern will be the mirror image of the final product!!

Foundation Piecing Steps

• Photocopy or trace the foundation piecing designs. If you choose to trace the designs, artist vellum works well.

• Trim away the excess paper from the copied design, leaving 1/4" beyond the outermost line.

• Cut a piece of background fabric for Section 1. The piece should be cut slightly larger than the area, allowing 1/4" for the seam allowance on all sides.

• Place the wrong side of fabric piece against the unmarked side of the foundation paper, position behind Section 1 and pin in place.

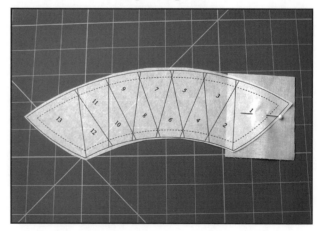

• Flip the assembly to expose the right side of fabric 1 and the unmarked side of the foundation paper.

• Cut a piece of fabric for Section 2. Allow 1/4" for the seam allowance on all sides. Position on top of Section 1 fabric, right sides together (r.s.t.).

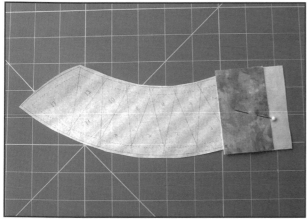

• Flip the paper/fabric assembly over. With the marked side of the foundation facing up, stitch on the seam line between sections 1 and 2. Stitch past the end of the seam line on either end to anchor the fabric. There is no need to back-tack, the stitches are small and will not be pulled out.

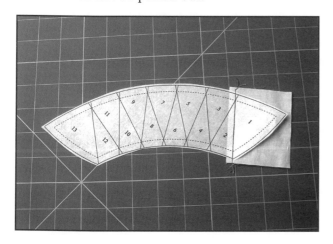

• Finger press the seam to eliminate all pleats or carefully press the seam using an iron without steam. This is a very important step. A poorly pressed seam may mean disaster later.

• Flip the paper/fabric assembly over to reveal the printed paper side again. Place a postcard along the seam line between Sections 2 and 3.

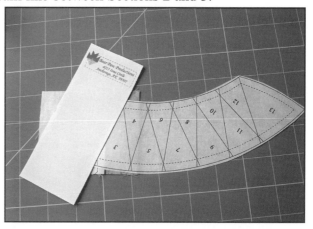

• Fold the paper over this stiff edge and cut away the excess fabric 1/4" from this folded edge. You may use any small ruler with 1/4" markings. I prefer to us an **Add-A-Quarter**™ ruler.

• Open the folded paper, and flip again to reveal the fabric pieces. Place fabric #3 in position, raw edges even with the newly cut edge, r.s.t.

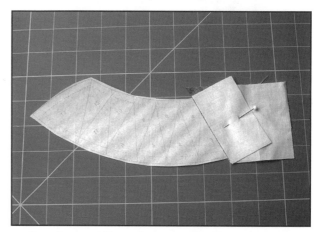

• Continue adding pieces until all sections have been completely covered. Trim the edge of the block along the outermost line, leaving a 1/4" seam allowance.

• After trimming, remove the foundation paper. Pinch the beginning of the seam between the thumb and forefinger of your "wrong" hand and gently pull away the paper, placing all excess force against the thumb nail holding the seam down. If removed in this manner, undue roughness will be reduced with stretching and pulled stitches kept to a minimum.

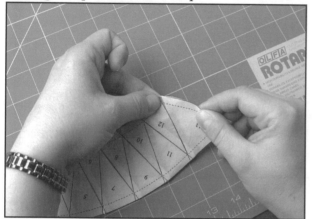

• Stitch the block units together after completing the paper pieced portion of the block construction.

Speedy Flying Geese

This method is most accurate when the fabrics involved have been starched to a firm finish.

• Cut the fabrics as follows:
Geese - Triangle A: cut the triangles as you normally would. The geese are cut from a square 1 1/4" larger than the finished products. The square is cut twice diagonally to yield 4 quarter square triangles.

finished size plus 1 1/4"

Background or Sky - Triangle B: cut the triangles from a square that is 1" larger than the cut size of the geese square. If the geese square is cut 5 1/4", cut the background square 6 1/4". Cut this square twice diagonally to yield 4 quarter square triangles.

geese size plus 1"

• Place each background Triangle B right side together with a Triangle A. The background triangle should be on top, with the square corner aligned. Stitch from the square corner to the point. Press the seam toward the background triangle.

• Pair units from above, align the points. The center seam allowances will not line up!! Stitch along the bias edge using the standard 1/4" seam allowance.

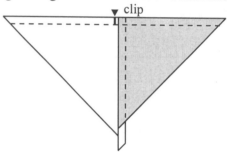

• Snip the seam allowance at the center of the long seam, **cut just through the sewing line**. This will allow the seam allowance to be split and pressed away from each of the geese triangles. The stitched and pressed unit will look like the diagrams below.

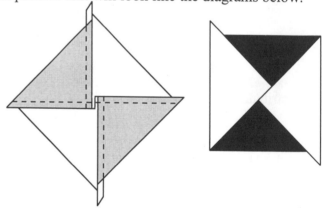

• Cut the unit in half as diagramed. This cutting line will be 1/4" from the tip of each geese triangle, thus preserving the integrity of your 1/4" seam allowance when stitching geese to another unit. The cutting line will also be at a 45° from the diagonal seam. This cut will yield two geese units from the original.

• Trim the excess background fabric from the right of each flying geese unit. This excess will measure 1/2" wide. TaDa, you have just constructed two flying geese! A trimming template has been included for your convenience, should you feel the need to use one.

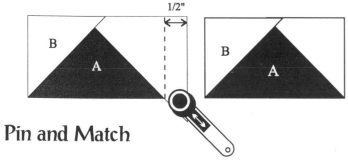

Pin and Match

My personal feeling about pins is that I will use them only when absolutely necessary. In most cases, seams can easily be stitched without the assistance of a pin. At other times, the pinning of seams is a necessary evil. If I feel that pins are important for a particular seam, I will instruct you to pin. The remainder of the time, pinning is up to your personal preference.

Opposing Seams - Generally, methods are employed to ensure that the seams match nicely without the use of pins. This method involves pressing the seams in such a manner that the seams oppose - i.e., the seams are laying in opposite directions. A seam that is pressed in one direction, creates a ridge. When seams oppose, we take advantage of those ridges and make the seams butt up against each other. This will also distribute the bulk of the seam.

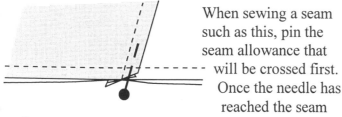

When sewing a seam such as this, pin the seam allowance that will be crossed first. Once the needle has reached the seam allowance, remove the pin. The seam should not shift at this point.

Do not sew over pins! If the sewing machine needle hits the pin, the machine can be damaged. The broken needle may fly into an unprotected eye!

Stab Through Pinning - This method is employed when very specific points must match. A pin is "stabbed" through the two points that must match, and anchored. As the units are sewn together, the

seam will pass through the point that the pin was securing.

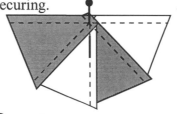 

Pressing

Seams are generally pressed toward one side, rather than open as in clothing construction. Most often the seam is pressed behind the darker fabric. BUT, all rules are made to be broken!! The instructions given in this book include precise pressing directions, generally in the form of arrows. Care has been taken to ensure that seams oppose if possible.

First press the seam flat from the wrong side. This smooths any puckers caused by thread tension problems. Then, open the layers, press from the right side, and watch for any pleating at the seam.

Pressing is a personal topic. Fabric prepared with spray starch can be finger pressed, although I would encourage frequent trips to the ironing board. Blocks that are steam pressed as they are sewn tend to lay flatter!

Swirled Seams - Because of the number of seams that will intersect in this quilt, it is even more important to press the seams so that they will oppose. To accomplish this, the seams of the Pinwheel and Quarter Square Triangle blocks will be pressed in one direction. After the block halves are sewn together, pull the two or three stitches of the vertical seam that extend past the long seam into the 1/4" seam allowance. This will allow the final seam to be swirled and pressed so that all of the seams are rotating in one direction, distributing the bulk in the center of the block.

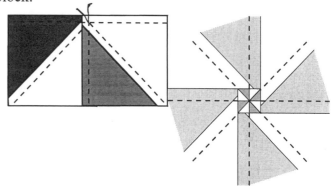

Stained Glass Applique

Foundation Preparation

• Cut the background fabric slightly larger than the full size pattern. The finished size of each design after all seams are sewn is 11" x 15". Cut the background fabric to 12 1/2" x 16 1/2".

• Center the background fabric over the pattern, and tape in place with masking tape. Trace the entire pattern on to the background fabric using a #2 pencil. If a line of the design extends to the edge of the paper, be sure to draw that line to the edge of the background fabric as you are drawing.

Basting Option #1
Fusible Web Preparation and Application

• Cut the fusible web to 12 1/2" x 16 1/2".

• Tape the pattern to a large window or light box with the **backside** of the pattern exposed. Tape the fusible web on top and trace the reversed pattern on to the paper side of the fusible web with a pencil. Trace the lines that extend to the edge of the pattern to the edge of the fusible web.

• Cut the fusible web exactly on the pencil lines with paper scissors. Do not add seam allowances. You may label each piece to simplify the assembly of the design.

• Adjacent pieces that are of the same fabric may be cut as one unit - such as leaf halves. Pay close attention to directional fabric. The resulting placement of a directional print may be undesirable.

• Press the fusible web pieces to the **wrong side** of the selected fabrics following the manufacturers directions. Avoid over pressing the fusible web at this stage, it may cause the paper to be difficult to remove.

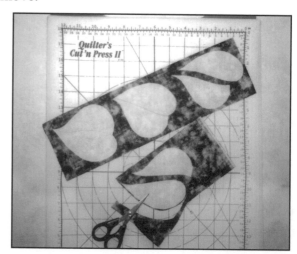

• Fabric grain lines are not important. Place fusible web in such a way as to make the best use of the fabric design.

• Cut the fabric slightly larger than the adhered fusible web - 1/16" extra will allow the fabric raw edges to overlap a little when fusing the pieces to the background.

• Remove the paper backing of the fusible web/fabric unit, and press in place on the background fabric.

• Be sure that the applique pieces are touching or overlapping a bit. Do not leave any gaps.

• Retrace any lines covered by the fabric applique pieces that have been cut as one unit - such a lines between the leaf halves. Use a pencil to retrace these lines.

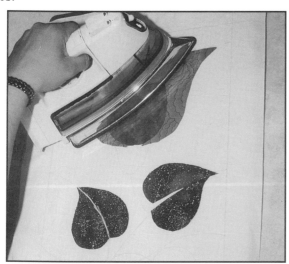

Basting Option #2
Freezer Paper Templates and Glue Basting

This is the method that I chose to use for this project. The finished blocks are softer and "fit" better with the pieced blocks that surround them.

The glue basted method also lends itself well to the needs of those who would rather hand stitch the leading in place.

• Cut the freezer paper to 12 1/2" x 16 1/2".

• Trace the entire pattern, **right side up**, on to the paper side of the freezer paper.

• Cut the freezer paper exactly on the pencil lines with paper scissors.

• Press the shiny side of the freezer paper to the **right side** of the selected fabrics using a warm iron.

• Cut the fabric slightly larger than the adhered freezer paper - 1/16" extra will allow the fabric raw edges to overlap a little when basting the pieces to the background.

• Remove the freezer paper from the cut fabric section.

• Place dots of basting glue on the foundation along the outline of the piece to be placed. Glue basting is diagramed below using **Roxanne's Glue-Baste-It!** Carefully position the fabric piece on the foundation. All dots of glue should be covered by the applied fabric. Allow the glue to dry.

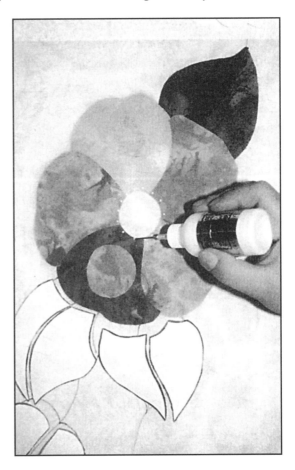

• Retrace any lines covered by the fabric applique pieces that have been cut as one unit - such as lines between the leaf halves. Use a pencil to retrace these lines.

Bias Tape Application

•The bias tape used in this project is a **Clover** product. This specific bias tape is used for a number of reasons:

1) **fusible web** has been applied to the wrong side of the bias tape, allowing all of the bias tape to be pressed in place on to the project before stitching begins,

2) this bias tape is 100% cotton,

3) it is slightly narrower than the standard bias tape available and very flexible, allowing tight curves to be negotiated, and

4) the fusible web allows the bias tape to be gently pulled from the design and repositioned for the desired results.

•The purpose of the bias tape is to cover the raw edges of all fabric pieces and to simulate stained glass leading.

•Bias tape will cover all raw edges of the applique. The bias tape is centered directly over the junction of the applique raw edges, over a single raw edge or over the drawn leading line.

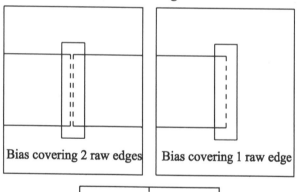

Bias covering 2 raw edges   Bias covering 1 raw edge

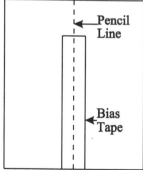

• All bias tape ends must be covered!! Be sure to plan ahead. First, place all bias tape lengths that do not cover another's raw end. **Lead all of the lines marked #1 first. Then go on to lead all of the lines marked #2.**

• Points - Miter the bias tape at each point. Press the fusible bias tape into place up to the point. Insert a pin into the edge of the bias tape where the point of the miter will be positioned. Pull the bias tape against this pin as you fold under the excess fabric, causing the mitered angle to form. In the case of a very sharp point, the fold may lay along the outer edge of the bias tape as shown below.

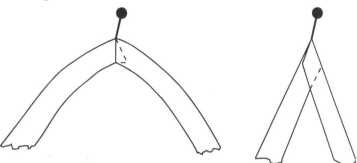

•If you find that you have accidentally applied a piece of bias tape before its time, carefully pull the bias tape away from the applique to release just enough space to insert the next bias tape end. You may use a pin to lift the prematurely placed bias tape from the design.

•The pattern may include bias tape intersections that are diagramed enclosed by a small box. The box indicates that the first piece of bias tape applied will need to be released from the design and another piece of bias tape inserted. Occasionally this cannot be avoided.

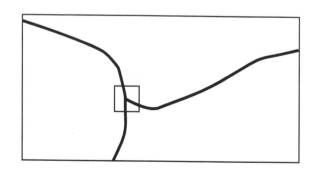

•Trim the end of the bias tape along the leading line that is intersected. This will allow the raw end of the bias tape to be covered (overlapped 1/8") by the next piece of bias tape. This may mean trimming the end of the bias tape at an unusual angle to accommodate the leading line.

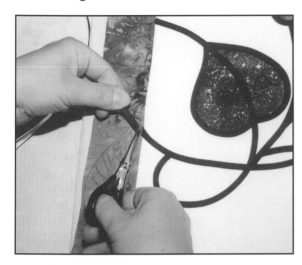

•If you have positioned a piece of bias tape badly, simply lift it from its place, reposition, and press in place with a warm iron.

Stitching Bias Tape In Place

•Insert a very fine needle into the sewing machine, size 60/8 works well. The holes left by the needle are very small, preventing the bobbin thread from popping to the surface.

•Thread the sewing machine needle with a fine black thread. Sew Bob (a fine lingerie thread), black embroidery thread, or silk thread work well. Fill the bobbin with black cotton thread.

• Use an open toe embroidery foot on your sewing machine, if you have one. It will be easier to see what you are doing.

•Stitch both edges of the bias tape in place using a straight stitch. Backstitch at both ends to secure the seam. Stitch at the very edge of the bias tape to avoid an unsightly pleat of bias tape that is not secured. Either side may be stitched first.

•Clip threads close to the surface - front and back of the block.

•Use a sewing awl to adjust and smooth bias tape if any puckering has occurred at tight curves.

•If any of the bias tape should loosen as you are working, it can be secured again by gently pressing it back in place.

Finishing Touches

After each block is stitched, you may find that it no longer lays absolutely flat. The tension of the thread as the background fabric is stitched across "randomly" causes the pucker to occur. It is for that very reason that machine embroidery artists use a stabilizer on the wrong side of the background fabric. You have two options to smooth this problem.

• Stitch each block with a stabilizer on the wrong side of your background fabric. The puckering is reduced if not entirely eliminated. The only drawback to this is the tedious paper removal after completion of the block.

• Each block can be "blocked" as you would a knit item. Draw a rectangle on your pressing surface that measures 12 1/2" x 16 1/2". Pin the edges of the block, right side down, to the drawn line. If the block has drawn up you will need to give a slight tug as you are pinning it in place to bring the fabric to the drawn line. Lightly mist the block and gently steam with your hot iron. Allow the block to dry and cool before you remove the pins.

TRIM each completed stained glass block to 11 1/2" x 15 1/2". Trimming the block will give a perfectly straight edge and remove any ragged, loose ends created as you stitch the bias tape in place.

Stained Glass Flower Garden

Finished Size 84" x 88"

Fabric Requirements

Background - assorted light tans - 7 yards
                  includes binding.
Stained Glass borders - 24 1" wide strips - 3/4 yards
Dark - assorted pieces in a range of color - 3 1/2 yards
Light - assorted pieces in a range of color - 3 yards

The yardage requirements for the stained glass applique has been included at left. Please refer to the individual blocks for specific requirements.

Yardage has been calculated generously to allow for variations due to multiple fabric use.

Pansy

Fabric Requirements

Background - rectangle 12 1/2" x 16 1/2"
  (will be trimmed to 11 1/2" x 15 1/2")
Leaves and Stem - 8" square
Purple - 6" x 14"

Yellow - 6" x 10"

Black Fusible Bias Tape - 4 yards

Bear Paw Productions
PO Box 230589 • Anchorage, AK 99523-0589
(907) 349-7873 • Phone (907) 349-7875 • FAX
www.bearpawproductions.com

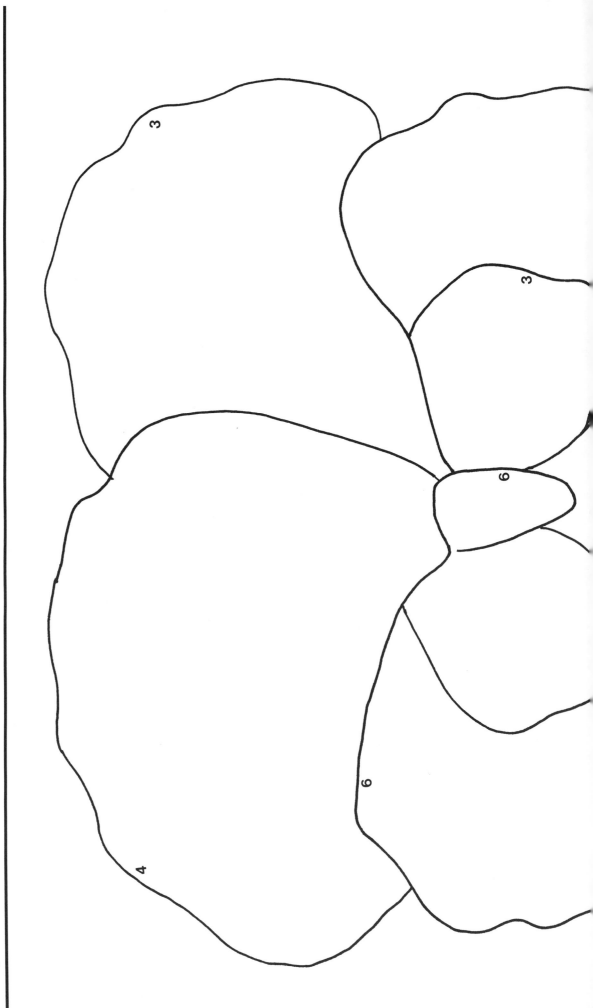

Waterlily

Fabric Requirements

Background - rectangle 12 1/2" x 16 1/2"
(will be trimmed to 11 1/2" x 15 1/2")
Leaves and Stems - 8" x 10" rectangle
Dark Pink - 12" x 5"

Medium Pink - 5" x 10"
Light Pink - 5" x 10"
White - 5" square
Black Fusible Bias Tape - 4 yards

Bear Paw Productions

PO Box 230589 • Anchorage, AK 99523-0589
(907) 349-7873 • Phone   (907) 349-7875 • FAX
www.bearpawproductions.com

Tulips

Fabric Requirements

Background - rectangle 12 1/2" x 16 1/2"
  (will be trimmed to 11 1/2" x 15 1/2")
Leaves and Stems - 2 pieces 6" x 14"
Red/Orange - 2 squares 6"

Yellow - 4" square

Black Fusible Bias Tape - 4 yards

Bear Paw Productions

PO Box 230589 • Anchorage, AK 99523-0589
(907) 349-7873 • Phone   (907) 349-7875 • FAX
www.bearpawproductions.com

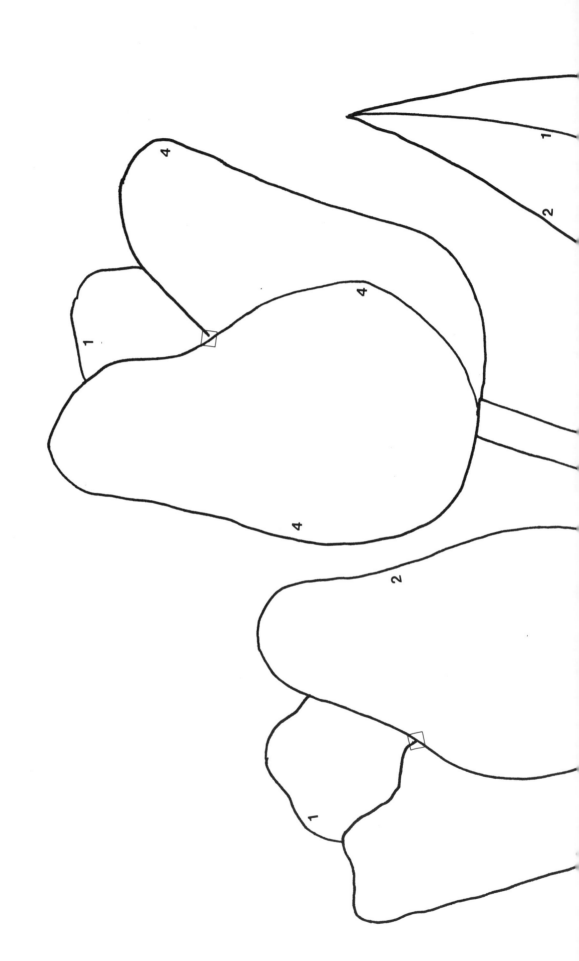

Calla Lily

Fabric Requirements

Background - rectangle 12 1/2" x 16 1/2"
(will be trimmed to 11 1/2" x 15 1/2")
Leaves and Stems - 3 pieces 5" x 8"
Dark Cream - 4" x 10"

Cream - 4" square
White - 4" x 8"
Yellow - 2" x 3"
Black Fusible Bias Tape - 4 yards

Bear Paw Productions

PO Box 230589 • Anchorage, AK 99523-0589
(907) 349-7873 • Phone   (907) 349-7875 • FAX
www.bearpawproductions.com

Sitka Rose

Fabric Requirements
Background - rectangle 12 1/2" x 16 1/2"
(will be trimmed to 11 1/2" x 15 1/2")

Leaves - 4 squares 5"

Pinks - 5 square 4"

Yellow - 2" square

Black Fusible Bias Tape - 3 yards

Bear Paw Productions
PO Box 230589 • Anchorage, AK 99523-0589
(907) 349-7873 • Phone   (907) 349-7875 • FAX
www.bearpawproductions.com

Poinsettia

Bear Paw Productions
PO Box 230589 • Anchorage, AK 99523-0589
(907) 349-7873 • Phone   (907) 349-7875 • FAX
www.bearpawproductions.com

Fabric Requirements

Background - rectangle 12 1/2" x 16 1/2"
(will be trimmed to 11 1/2" x 15 1/2")

Leaves and Stems - 4" x 20"

Red - 2 squares 10"

Center - 2" square

Black Fusible Bias Tape - 4 yards

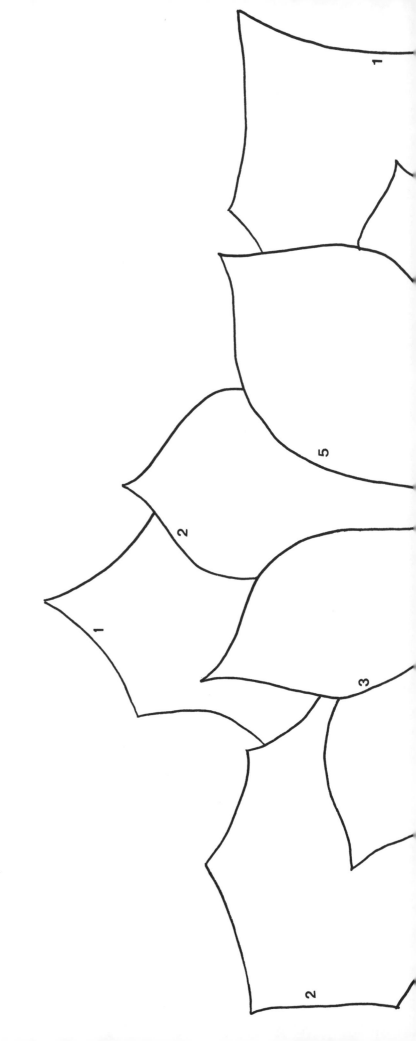

Sunflower

Fabric Requirements

Background - rectangle 12 1/2" x 16 1/2"
(will be trimmed to 11 1/2" x 15 1/2")
Leaves and Stems - 3 pieces 4" x 7"
Gold - 8 assorted pieces 3" x 10"

Brown Center - 2 squares 7"

Black Fusible Bias Tape - 5 yards

Bear Paw Productions

PO Box 230589 • Anchorage, AK 99523-0589
(907) 349-7873 • Phone (907) 349-7875 • FAX
www.bearpawproductions.com

Daffodil

Fabric Requirements
Background - rectangle 12 1/2" x 16 1/2"
    (will be trimmed to 11 1/2" x 15 1/2")
Leaves - 6" x 16 1/2"
Stem - 5" x 9"

Yellow - 2 squares 8"

Black Fusible Bias Tape - 4 yards

Bear Paw Productions
PO Box 230589 • Anchorage, AK 99523-0589
(907) 349-7873 • Phone   (907) 349-7875 • FAX
www.bearpawproductions.com

Hibiscus

Fabric Requirements

Background - rectangle 12 1/2" x 16 1/2"
(will be trimmed to 11 1/2" x 15 1/2")
Leaves - 2 squares 8"
Petals - 12" square

Yellow - 2" x 8"

Black Fusible Bias Tape - 4 yards

Bear Paw Productions

PO Box 230589 • Anchorage, AK 99523-0589
(907) 349-7873 • Phone   (907) 349-7875 • FAX
www.bearpawproductions.com

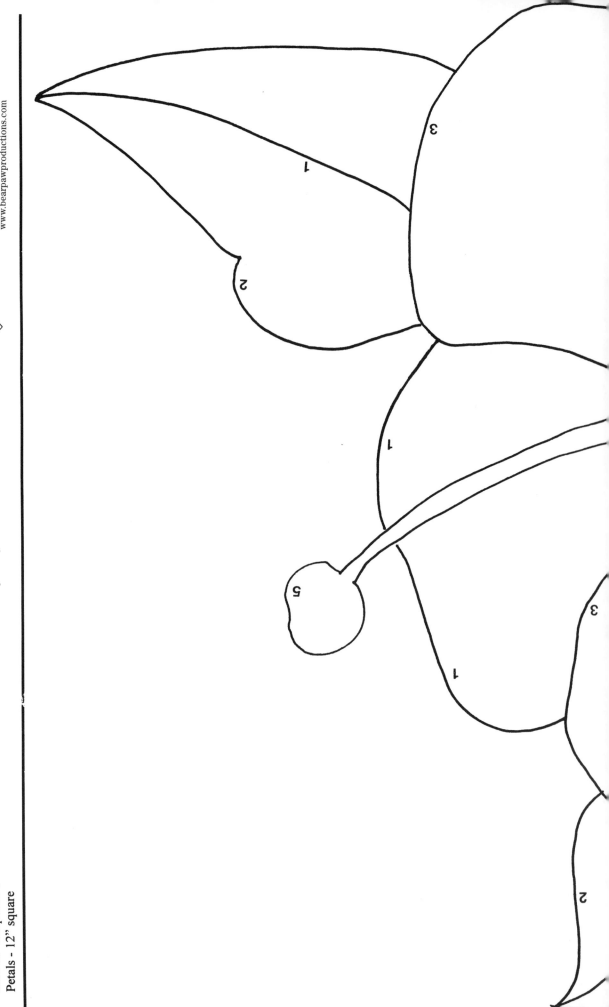

Aster

Bear Paw Productions

PO Box 230589 • Anchorage, AK 99523-0589
(907) 349-7873 • Phone   (907) 349-7875 • FAX
www.bearpawproductions.com

Fabric Requirements

Background - rectangle 12 1/2" x 16 1/2"
(will be trimmed to 11 1/2" x 15 1/2")
Leaves - 2 squares 6"
Purple - 3 squares 8"

Yellow - 3 squares 2"

Black Fusible Bias Tape - 6 yards

Fuchsia

Bear Paw Productions

PO Box 230589 • Anchorage, AK 99523-0589
(907) 349-7873 • Phone   (907) 349-7875 • FAX
www.bearpawproductions.com

Fabric Requirements
Background - rectangle 12 1/2" x 16 1/2"
    (will be trimmed to 11 1/2" x 15 1/2")
Leaves - 2 pieces 4" x 10"
Dark Pink - 3" x 7 1/2"
Medium Pink - 4" x 7"
Light Pink - 5" x 7"
Black Fusible Bias Tape - 4 yards
Dark Pink rayon thread to stitch stamen detail

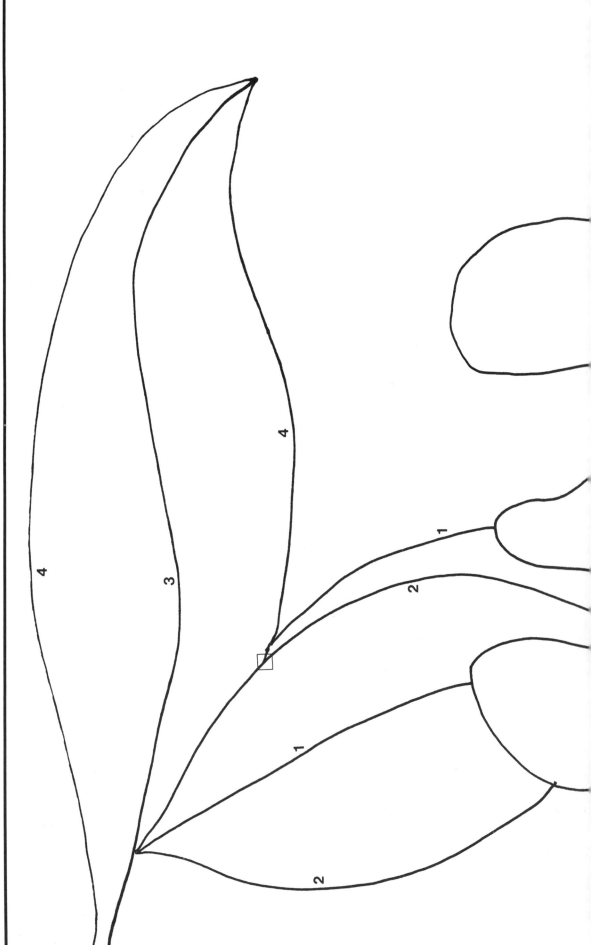

Butterfly

Fabric Requirements

Background - rectangle 12 1/2" x 16 1/2"
   (will be trimmed to 11 1/2" x 15 1/2")
Dark Purple - 10" square
Light Wing - 11" x 7"

Black Fusible Bias Tape - 2 1/2 yards

Black rayon thread to stitch antenna detail

Bear Paw Productions

PO Box 230589 • Anchorage, AK 99523-0589
(907) 349-7873 • Phone   (907) 349-7875 • FAX
www.bearpawproductions.com

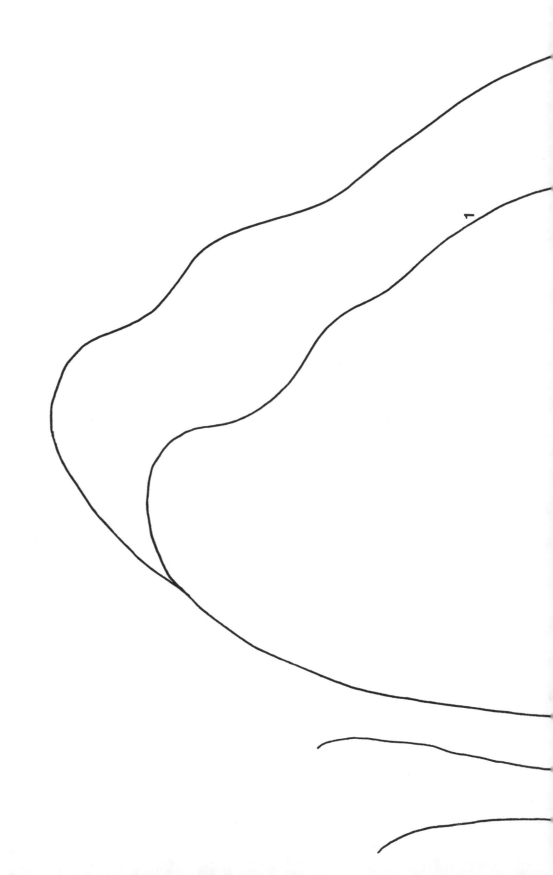

1

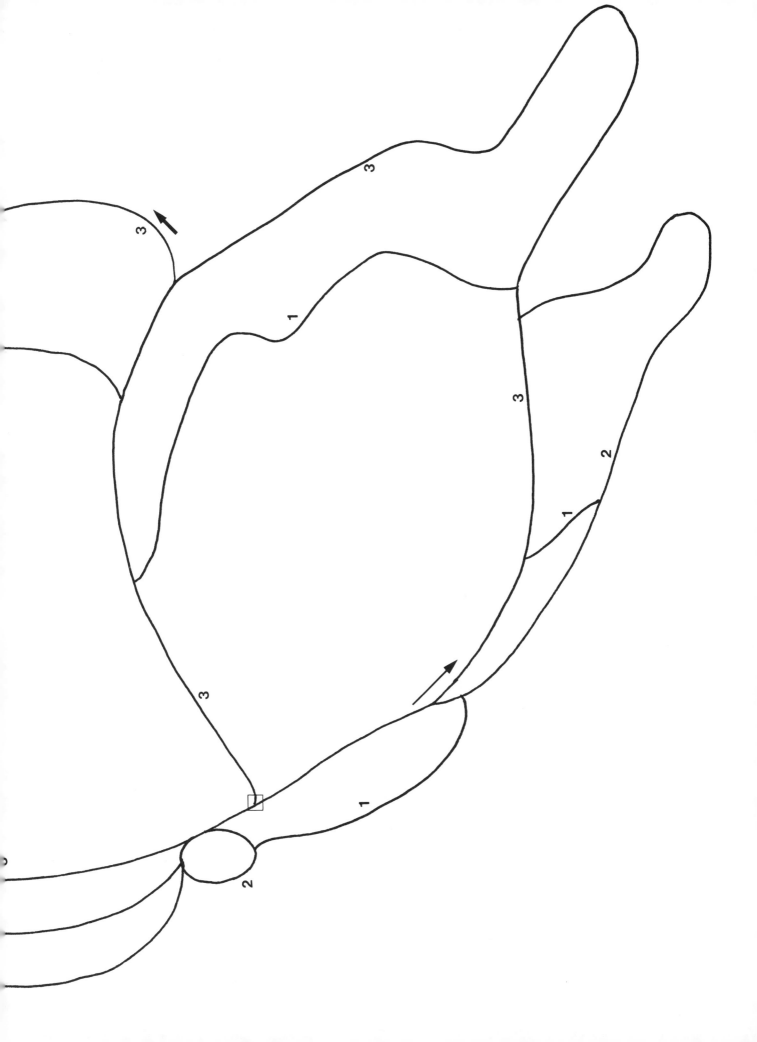

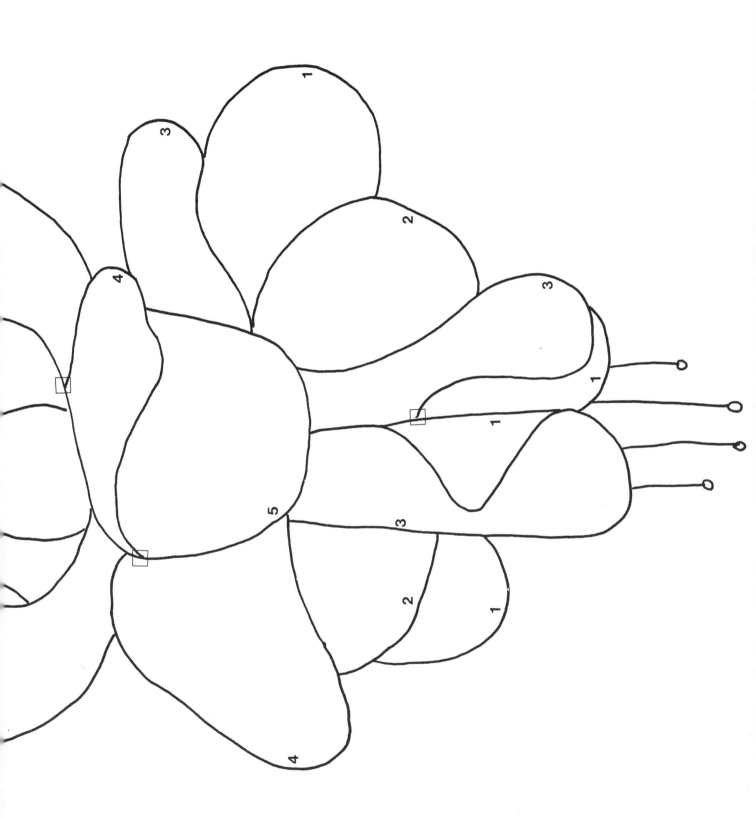

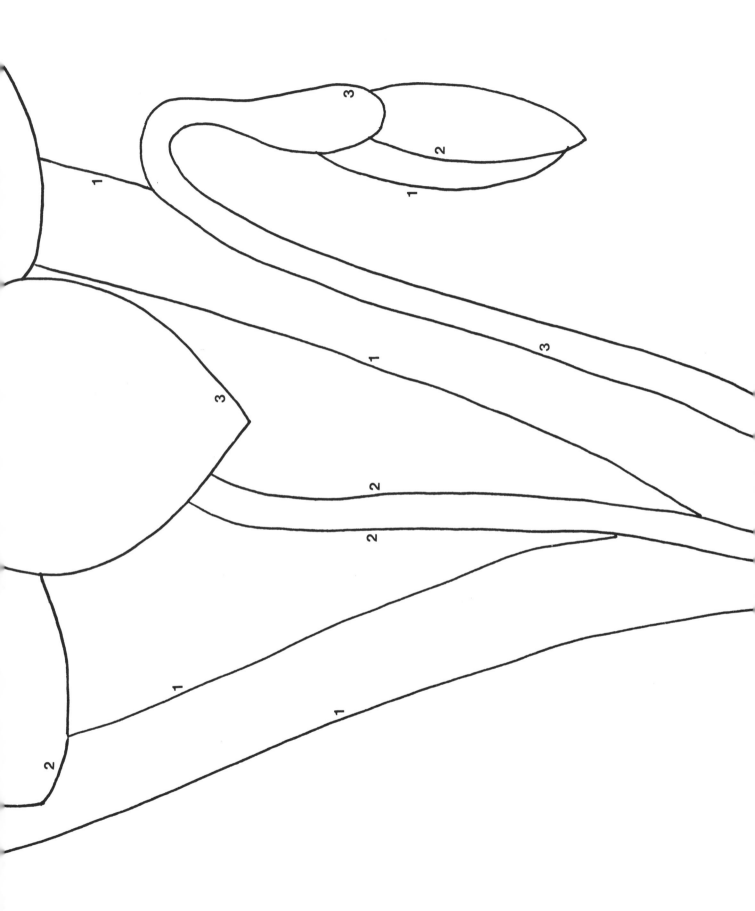

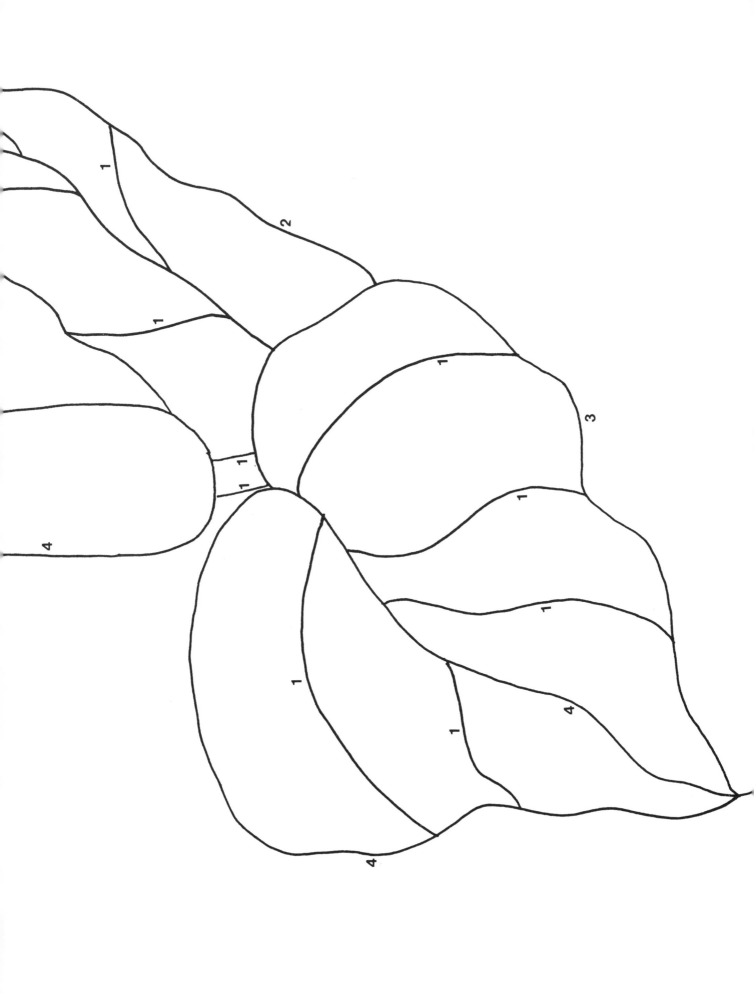

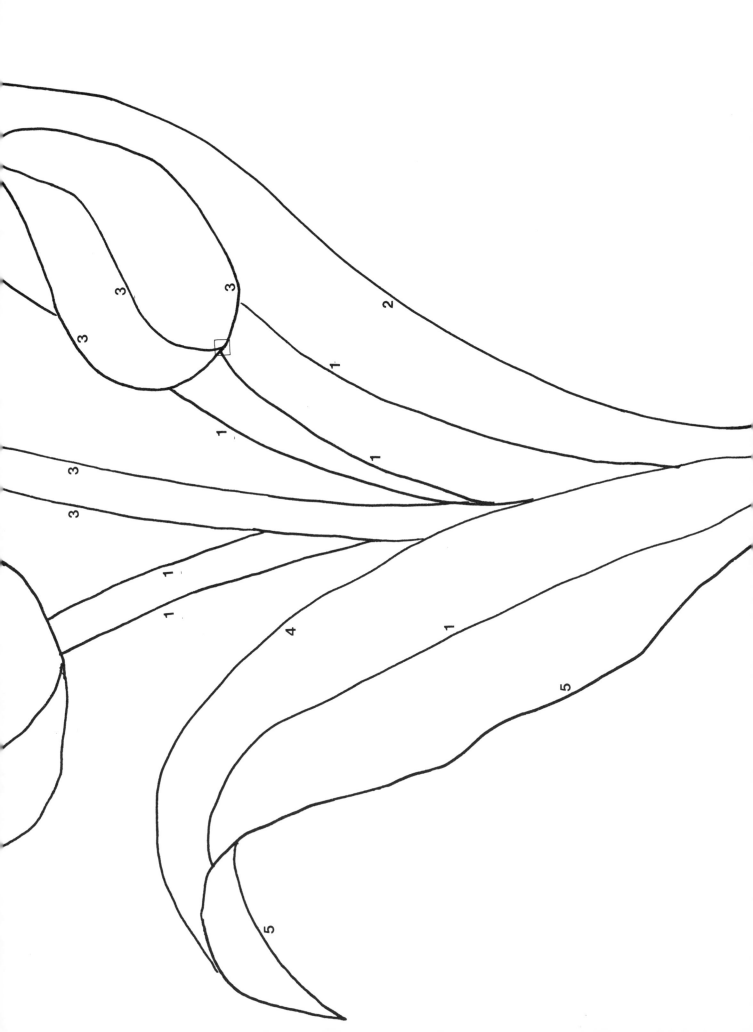

Stained Glass Flower Garden Quilt

Stained Glass Block Construction

Background Fabric
- Cut 4 strips 16 1/2"
    - cut strips into 12 rectangles 12 1/2" x 16 1/2"

Center and trace a stained glass design on to each background rectangle using a pencil. Apply the stained glass designs following the directions given on pages 12-15.

Gently block each completed stained glass design and trim to 11 1/2" x 15 1/2".

Cut the border strips in lengths to fit each stained glass block.

Cut 2   15 1/2" x 1" - sides
Cut 2   12 1/2" x 1" - top and bottom

Stitch the border strips to each side of the stained glass block. Apply the sides first and then the top and bottom. Press all seams toward the border strips.

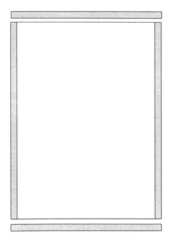 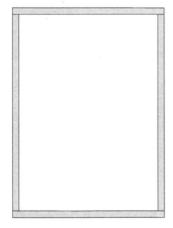

Pieced Block Construction

Sawtooth Star Variation
make 2 blocks - 8 1/2" square (8" finished)

Cutting Instructions - for one block. Construct two blocks using different color families.

Background	8 squares 2 1/2"
	1 square 5 1/4" cut twice diagonally
Color 1	4 squares 2 7/8" cut once diagonally
Color 2	1 square 4 1/2" - center square

Block Construction

#1 Place a 2 1/2" square of background fabric in one corner of the 4 1/2" square of Color 2 fabric. Stitch from corner to corner of the background square as diagramed. Trim the seam to 1/4" and press the seam toward the background triangle. Repeat this step until all corners of the 4 1/2" Color 2 square have a background triangle attached. The resulting unit will measure 4 1/2" from raw edge to raw edge.

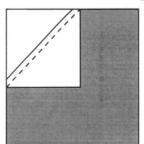 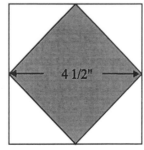

#2 Place a 2 7/8" half square triangle of Color 1 fabric right sides together on the corner of a 5 1/4" background quarter square triangle. Stitch the seam as indicated. Press the seam toward the Color 1 triangle. Make 4 identical units.

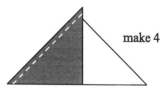
make 4

#3 Stitch the remaining 2 7/8" triangles on to the units. Start stitching at the 1/4" notch as shown below. Press the seam toward the Color 1 triangle. This unit will measure 2 1/2" x 4 1/2". Make 4.

Quarter inch notch

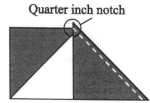

#4 Assemble the block as diagramed below. Press the seams as indicated by the arrows.

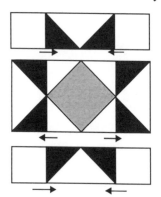
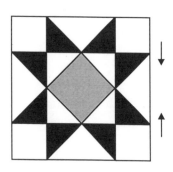

Yankee Puzzle

make 2 blocks - 8 1/2" square (8" finished)

Cutting Instructions - for one block. Construct two blocks using different color families.

Background	8 squares 2 7/8" - cut once diagonally
Color 1	2 squares 2 7/8" - cut once diagonally
	1 square 5 1/4" - cut twice diagonally
Color 2	2 squares 2 7/8" - cut once diagonally

18

Block Construction

#1 Stitch each 2 7/8" half square triangle of Color 1 fabric and Color 2 fabric to a 2 7/8" half square triangle of Background fabric. Press the seam toward the Colored fabric. Make 4 of each color.

make 4   make 4

#2 Stitch each Color 1 half square triangle unit to a Color 2 half square triangle unit. Pay careful attention to the diagram below for color placement. Press the seam toward the Color 1 unit. The finished unit will measure 2 1/2" x 4 1/2". Make 4.

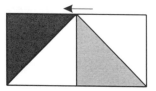

#3 Place a 2 7/8" half square triangle of Background fabric right sides together on the corner of a 5 1/4" Color 1 quarter square triangle. Stitch the seam as indicated. Press the seam toward the Background triangle. Make 4 identical units.

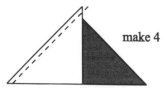
make 4

#4 Stitch the remaining 2 7/8" triangles on to the units as shown below. Press the seam toward the Background triangle. This unit will measure 2 1/2" x 4 1/2". Make 4 flying geese units.

Quarter inch notch

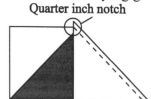

#5 Stitch each unit from step #2 to a unit from step #4. Press the seam toward the flying geese unit. Make 4.

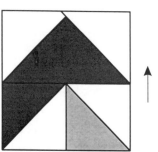

#6 Assemble the block as diagramed below. Press the seams as indicated by the arrows.

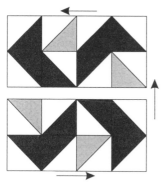

Note Leave one of the blocks constructed in quarter block units. This is necessary because of the quilt top construction order.

Dark Pinwheels

make 19 blocks - 4 1/2" square (4" finished)

Cutting Instructions

Background   10 squares 6 1/4"
Dark Colors   10 squares 6 1/4"

Block Construction

#1 Photocopy or trace 10 half square triangle foundation papers. The paper used will be two squares long by two squares wide.

#2 Place a 6 1/4" square of Background fabric right sides together with a 6 1/4" square of Dark fabric. Construct half square triangle units following the triangle foundation method detailed on page 7. Press the seam toward the Dark fabric. Each pair will yield eight half square triangle units measuring 2 1/2".

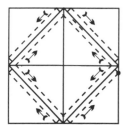
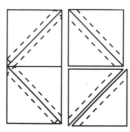

Note If you wish to piece the triangles in the traditional method (triangle to triangle), cut each 6 1/4" square into four 2 7/8" squares - cut each 2 7/8" square once diagonally.

#3 Stitch half square triangle units together. Press the seam toward the background triangle. Stitch each sewn pair to a second pair as diagramed.

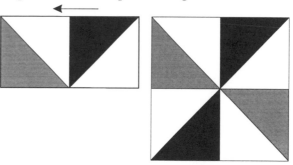

#4 Pull the two or three stitches of the vertical seam that extend past the long seam into the 1/4" seam allowance. This will allow the final seam to be swirled and pressed so that all seam allowances are rotating in the same direction, distributing the bulk in the center of the block. This has a second benefit - it creates opposing seam allowances when sewing blocks together. The amount of fabric cut and pieced will produce 20 Dark Pinwheel blocks, only 19 are required.

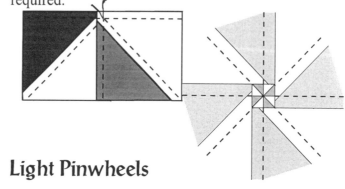

Light Pinwheels

make 69 blocks - 4 1/2" square (4" finished)

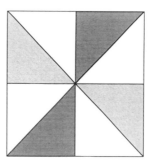

Cutting Instructions

Background   35 squares 6 1/4"
Light Colors   35 squares 6 1/4"

Block Construction

#1 Photocopy or trace 35 half square triangle foundation papers. The paper used will be two squares long by two squares wide.

#2 Place a 6 1/4" square of Background fabric right sides together with a 6 1/4" square of Light fabric. Construct half square triangle units following the triangle foundation method detailed on page 7. Press the seam toward the light fabric. Each pair will yield eight half square triangle units measuring 2 1/2".

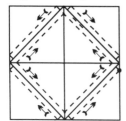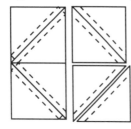

Note If you wish to piece the triangles in the traditional method (triangle to triangle), cut each 6 1/4" square into four 2 7/8" squares - cut each 2 7/8" square once diagonally.

#3 Stitch half square triangle units together. Press the seam toward the Background triangle. Stitch each sewn pair to a second pair as diagramed.

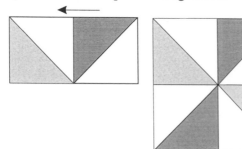

#4 Pull the two or three stitches of the vertical seam that extend past the long seam into the 1/4" seam allowance, and swirl the seam allowances. The amount of fabric cut and pieced will produce 70 Light Pinwheel blocks, only 69 are required.

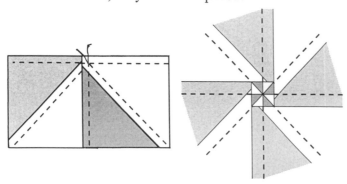

Quarter Square Triangle Blocks
make 58 blocks - 4 1/2" square (4" finished)

Cutting Instructions

Background	30 squares 5 1/2"
Light Colors	30 squares 5 1/2"

Block Construction

#1 Photocopy or trace 30 quarter square triangle foundation papers.

#2 Place a 5 1/2" square of Background fabric right sides together with a 5 1/2" square of Light fabric. Construct quarter square triangle units following the quarter square triangle foundation method detailed on page 8. Press the seam toward the Light fabric.

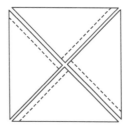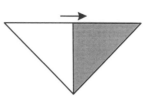

Note If you wish to piece the triangles in the traditional method, cut each square to 5 1/4". Cut each square twice diagonally to create quarter square triangles. Stitch quarter square triangles together.

#3 Stitch triangle pairs from step #2 together to complete the blocks.

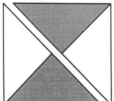

#4 Pull the two or three stitches of the vertical seam that extend past the long seam into the 1/4" seam allowance. Swirl the seams as you press. 60 blocks will be produced, only 58 are required.

20

Pieced Border Blocks

78 border blocks - 4 1/2" square (4" finished)
4 corner blocks - 4 1/2" squares (4" finished)

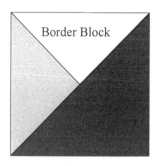 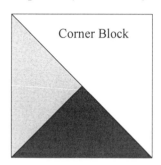

Border Block   Corner Block

Cutting Instructions

Background	20 squares 5 1/2"
	2 squares 4 7/8" - cut once diagonally
Dark Color	40 squares 4 7/8" - cut once diagonally
	1 square 5 1/4" - cut twice diagonally
Light Color	20 squares 5 1/2"
	1 square 5 1/4" - cut twice diagonally

Border Block Construction

#1 Photocopy or trace 20 quarter square triangle foundation papers.

#2 Place a 5 1/2" square of Background fabric right sides together with a 5 1/2" square of Light fabric. Construct quarter square triangle units following the quarter square triangle foundation method detailed on page 8. Press the seam toward the Light fabric.

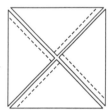

Note If you wish to piece the triangles in the traditional method, cut each square to 5 1/4". Cut each square twice diagonally to create quarter square triangles. Stitch quarter square triangles together.

#3 Stitch each triangle unit from step #2 to a 4 7/8" half square triangle of Dark Fabric to complete the border blocks. Press the seam toward the Dark triangle. 80 blocks will be produced, only 78 are required.

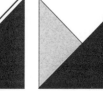

Corner Block Construction

#1 Stitch each 5 1/4" quarter square triangle of Dark fabric to a 5 1/4" quarter square triangle of Light fabric. Press the seam toward the Dark triangle.

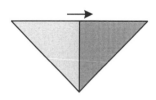

#2 To each unit from step #1 stitch a 4 7/8" half square triangle of Background fabric. Press the seam toward the Background triangle. Make 4.

Flying Geese

38 blocks - 2 1/2" x 4 1/2" (2" x 4" finished)

Cutting Instructions

Background	10 squares 6 1/4"	
		- cut twice diagonally
Dark Colors	10 squares 5 1/4"	
		- cut twice diagonally

Block Construction

#1 Stitch each Dark triangle to a Background triangle. Press the seam toward the Background triangle.

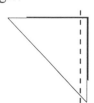 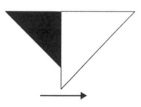

#2 Follow the directions given on page 10 to complete the flying geese units. 40 geese will be produced, only 38 are required.

21

Granny's Geese
16 geese - 2 1/2" x 4 1/2" (2" x 4" finished)

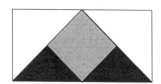

Cutting Instructions

Background	4 squares 6 1/4" - cut twice diagonally
Dark Color	8 squares 3 3/4" - cut once diagonally
Light Color	4 squares 3 7/8"

Block Construction

#1 Photocopy or trace 4 of the foundation paper templates below. Paper piece the unit following the paper piecing directions found on page 8. Trim on the outer solid line and cut the resulting square twice diagonally on the drawn line. Remove the foundation paper. Each will yield 4 Granny's Geese.

#2 Add the Background fabric to complete the blocks following the directions given on page 10. 16 Granny's Geese will be produced

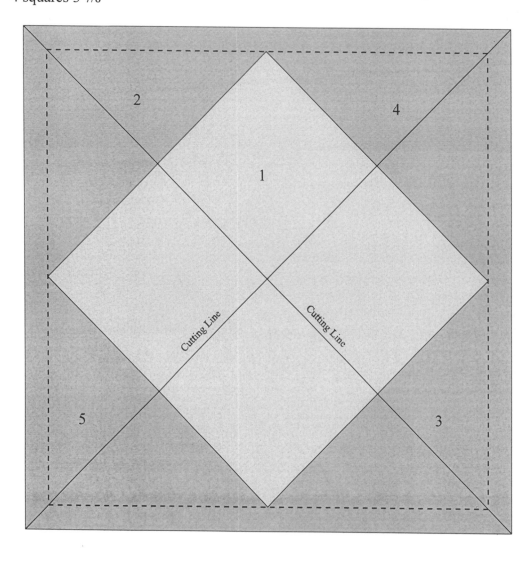

Granny's Halfsquare Geese
14 geese - 2 1/2" x 4 1/2" (2" x 4" finished)

Cutting Instructions

Background	4 squares 6 1/4" - cut twice diagonally
	8 squares 2 3/4" - cut once diagonally
Dark Color	8 squares 3 3/4" - cut once diagonally
	4 squares 3 1/4"

Block Construction

#1 Photocopy or trace 4 of the foundation paper templates below. Paper piece the unit following the paper piecing directions found on page 8. Trim on the outer solid line and cut the resulting square twice diagonally on the drawn line. Remove the foundation paper. Each will yield 4 Granny's Halfsquare Geese.

#2 Complete the blocks following the directions given on page 10. 16 Granny's Halfsquare Geese will be produced, only 14 blocks are required.

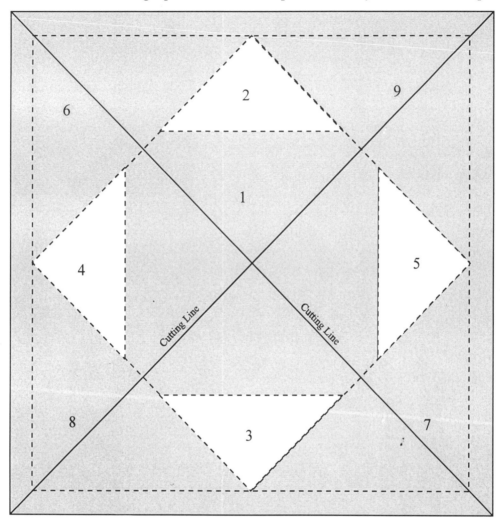

Flying Geese Trimming Template

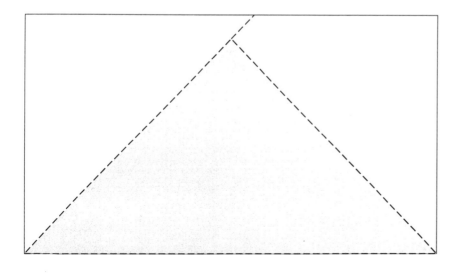

23

Northumberland Star

make 2 blocks - 8 1/2" square (8" finished)

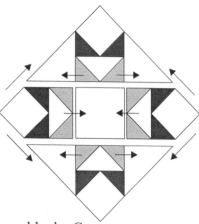

Cutting Instructions - for one block. Construct two blocks using different color families.

Background	1 square 5 1/4" - cut twice diagonally
	1 square 4 1/4" - cut twice diagonally
	1 square 3 3/8"
Color 1	4 squares 2 3/4" - cut once diagonally
Color 2	4 squares 2 3/4" - cut once diagonally

Block Construction

#1 Photocopy or trace 8 of the foundation at the right, and foundation paper piece the eight units following the directions given on page 8.

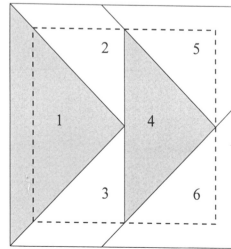

#2 Assemble the blocks using the cut background pieces and the foundation pieced units. Press as indicated by the arrows.

Wild Goose Chase

make 4 blocks - 4 1/2" square (4" finished)

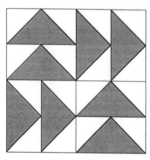
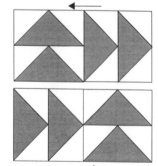

Cutting Instructions - for one block. Construct four blocks using different color families.

Background	8 squares 2 1/2" - cut once diagonally
Colors	2 squares 3 3/4" - cut twice diagonally

Block Construction

#1 Photocopy or trace 16 of the foundation below, and foundation paper piece the 16 units following the directions given on page 8.

#2 Assemble the blocks. Press as indicated by the arrows.

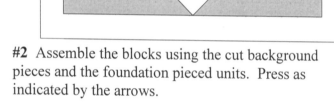

Log Cabin World Without End

make 1 block - 8 1/2" square (8" fin.)

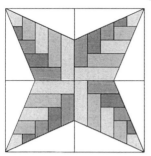

Fabric Selection

Background	pieces 10 and 11
Assorted Fabrics	pieces 1-9

Block Construction

#1 Photocopy or trace 4 of the foundation at the right, and foundation paper piece the eight units following the directions given on page 8.

#2 Assemble the block.

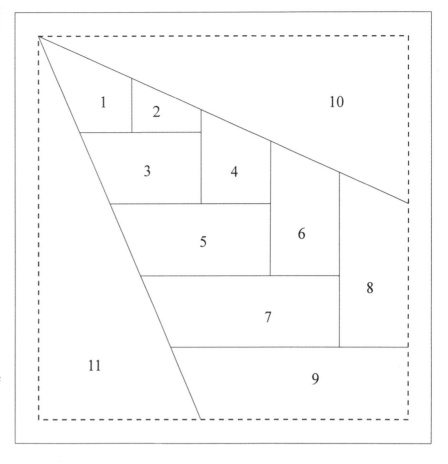

Starry World Without End

make 1 block - 8 1/2" square (8" fin.)

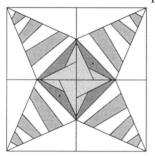

Fabric Selection

Background	pieces 11 and 12
Assorted Fabrics	pieces 1-8
Yellow Star	pieces 9 and 10

Block Construction

#1 Photocopy or trace 4 of the foundation at the right, and foundation paper piece the eight units following the directions given on page 8.

#2 Assemble the block.

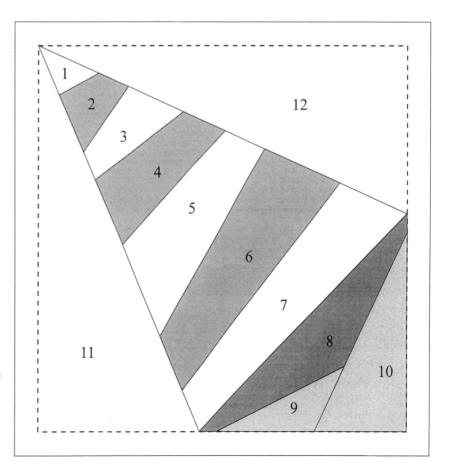

Feathered World Without End

make 1 block - 8 1/2" square (8" fin.)

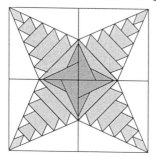

Fabric Selection

Color 1   pieces 1, 4, 7, 10, 13 and 16
Blue Star   pieces 17 and 18

Block Construction

#1 Photocopy or trace 4 of the foundation at the right, and foundation paper piece the eight units following the directions given on page 8.

#2 Assemble the block.

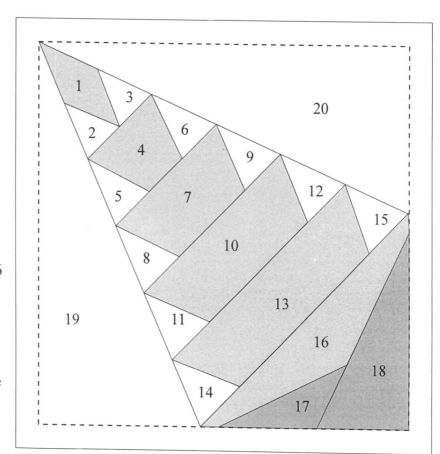

Northern Lights

make 2 blocks - 8 1/2" square (8" fin.)

Block Construction

#1 Photocopy or trace 8 of each foundation at the right, and foundation paper piece the 16 units following the directions given on page 8.

#2 Stitch each Unit A to a Unit B. Press the seam toward Unit A.

#3 Assemble one block completely. Swirl the final seam.

Note Leave one block in quarters for quilt top construction.

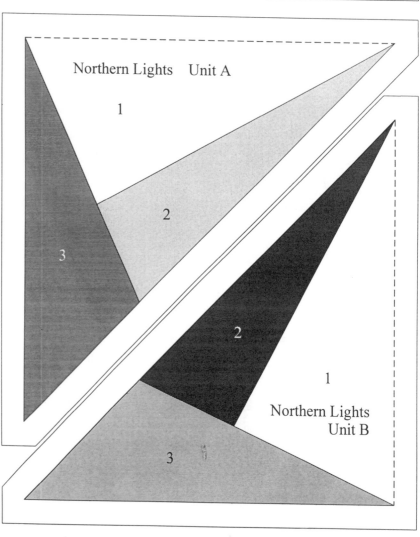

Queen Victoria's Crown

make 2 blocks - 8 1/2" square (8" finished)

Cutting Instructions - for one block. Construct two blocks using different color families.

Color 2 squares 3 7/8" - cut once diagonally
  1 squares 2 1/2"

Block Construction

#1 Photocopy or trace 4 of each unit, and foundation paper piece the units following the directions given on page 8.

#2 Assemble the block following the diagram below.

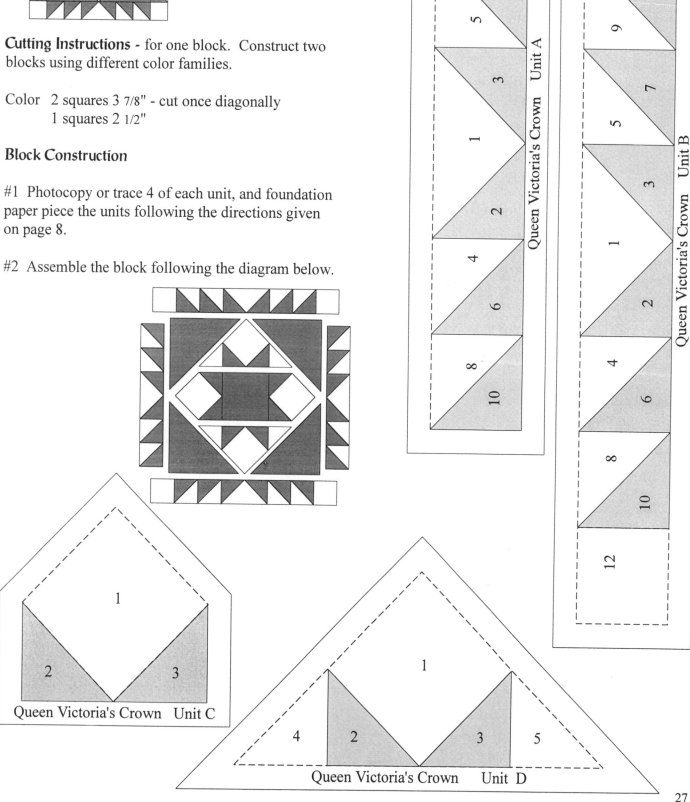

Queen Victoria's Crown   Unit A

Queen Victoria's Crown   Unit B

Queen Victoria's Crown   Unit C

Queen Victoria's Crown   Unit D

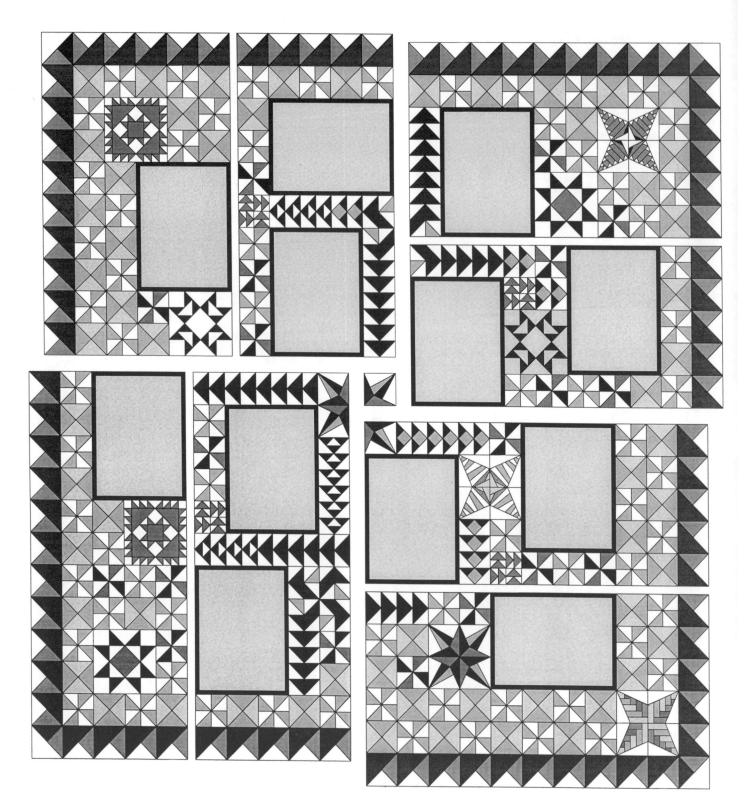

Quilt Top Assembly

#1 Arrange the pieced and stained glass blocks on a design wall to determine where you would like to place the blocks. The diagram above shows where the blocks were placed in the model quilt. Please feel free to arrange your blocks in a way that is pleasing to you and compliments your fabric choices.

#2 Notice that the Northern Lights block in the center

of the quilt top is broken into 1/4 block sections. One Yankee Puzzle block is also broken into quarters. This is to allow complete seams wherever possible to avoid set in seaming.

#3 Construct the quilt top in eighths and then quarters. The final seams are started with a partial seam between the 1/4 Northern Lights block and 1/4 quilt top portion. Follow the numbered seam directions below to complete the quilt top.

Half Square Triangle Foundation

2" half square triangles - 2 1/2" when measured from raw edge to raw edge

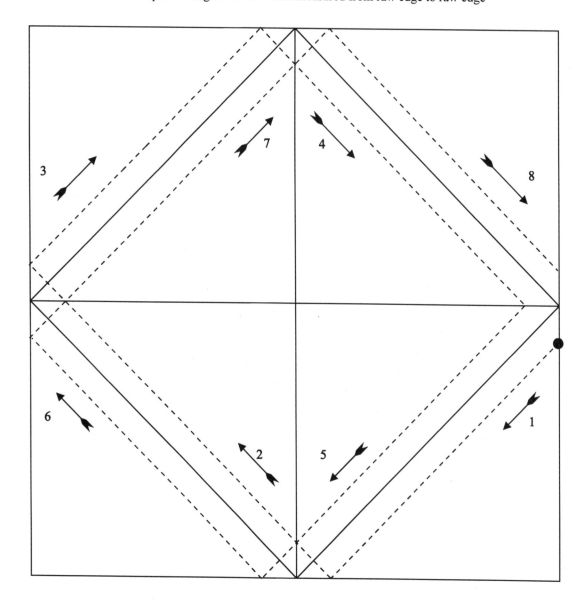

Quarter Square Triangle Foundation

4 1/2" when measured from raw edge to raw edge

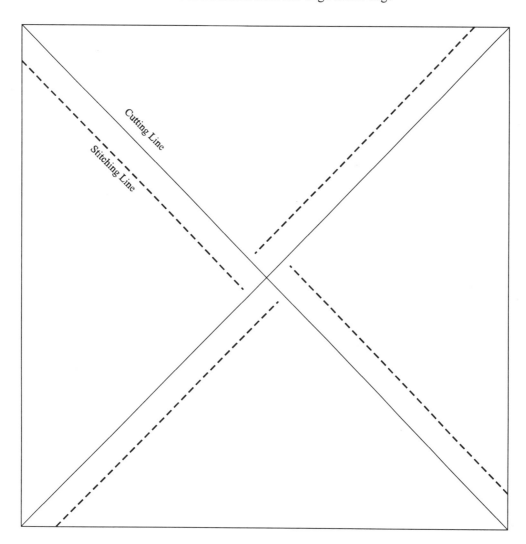

Foundation Copying Instructions

Foundation	Page	Copies	Foundation	Page	Copies
Half Square Triangle	30	45	Log Cabin World Without End	25	4
Quarter Square Triangle	31	50	Starry World Without End	25	4
Granny's Geese	22	4	Feathered World Without End	26	4
Granny's Halfsquare Geese	23	4	Northern Lights	26	8 of each
Northumberland Star	24	8	Queen Victoria's Crown	27	4 of each
Wild Goose Chase	24	16			

Other Books and Patterns by Brenda Henning

Books

Alaskan Silhouette Sampler
Among Friends ~ More Scrap Quilts
Christmas Traditions in Stained Glass
Birds of a Feather
Striptease ~ Stripping for Beginners
Early Bloomers in Stained Glass
Butterfly Kisses
Indian Summer
Sampler Schoolhouse ~ Second Edition

Stained Glass Patterns

Hummingbird
Wild Roses
Wild Poppies
Wild Iris
Forget-Me-Not
Fireweed
Calla Lily
Sunflower
Hibiscus
Heralding Angel

Clover Quick Bias

available in black, gold, silver, black lame' and copper

These books, patterns and Clover Quick Bias
are available at your local shop or from:

Bear Paw Productions
PO Box 230589
Anchorage, AK   99523-0589
Phone (907) 349-7873
FAX (907) 349-7875
www.bearpawproductions.com

Sources

Specialty products used in the text are listed below. Please check with your local quilt shop for availability of the product before you contact the manufacturer directly. Support your local shop!

TRIANGLES ON A ROLL
Gridded Half Square Triangle Paper
  Dutton Designs
  P.O. Box 7646
  Chandler, AZ 85246-7646

TRIANGLE PAPER™
  SPPS, Inc./Quiltime
  4410 N. Rancho Dr., #165
  Las Vegas, NV 89130

ADD-A-QUARTER RULER™
  CM Designs
  10669 Singleleaf Ct.
  Parker, CO 80134
  (303)841-5920

ROXANNE'S GLUE-BASTE-IT!™
  Roxanne Products Company
  742 Granite Ave
  Lathrop, CA 95330